Read-About® Holidays

Earth Day

By David F. Marx

Consultant
Katharine A. Kane, Reading Specialist
Former Language Arts Coordinator
San Diego County Office of Education

Children's Press®
A Division of Grolier Publishing
New York London Hong Kong Sydney
Danbury, Connecticut

Visit Children's Press® on the Internet at:
http://publishing.grolier.com

Designer: Herman Adler Design
Photo Researcher: Caroline Anderson

Library of Congress Cataloging-in-Publication Data

Marx, David F.
　　Earth Day / by David F. Marx.
　　　　p. cm. — (Rookie read-about holidays)
　　Includes index.
　　Summary: Introduces the holiday Earth Day, discussing its purpose
and how it is celebrated.
　　ISBN 0-516-22231-7 (lib. bdg.)　　　0-516-27174-1 (pbk.)
　　1. Earth Day—Juvenile literature. 2. Environmental policy—United
States—Juvenile literature. 3. Environmental protection—United States—
Juvenile literature. [1. Earth Day. 2. Environmental protection.
3. Holidays.] I. Title. II. Series.
GE180.M37　　2001
333.7—dc21
　　　　　　　　　　　　　　　　　　　00-026999

GROLIER
PUBLISHING　　　3 4 5 6 7 8 9 10 R 10 09 08 07 06 05 04 03 02

Earth Day is a holiday
when we celebrate
the environment
(en-VIE-ruhn-ment).

What is the environment?
Just look around!

The ground, water, air, plants, and animals all make up the environment.

A clean environment helps people stay healthy. People need to drink clean water, breathe clean air, and eat food that grows in clean soil. People can get sick if the environment is dirty.

How does the environment get dirty?

Cars and factories fill the air with smog.

Smog can make it hard for people to breathe.

Garbage pollutes
(puh-LOOTS), or dirties,
the water and soil.

Plants and animals cannot
grow well because of
the garbage.

Gaylord Nelson started
Earth Day in 1970.

He wanted to save the
environment.

Mr. Nelson taught people
about the things that hurt
our land, water, and air.

13

April 2001

Sunday	Monday	Tuesday	Wednesday	Thursday	Friday	Saturday
1	2	3	4	5	6	7
8	9	10	11	12	13	14
15	16	17	18	19	20	21
22	23	24	25	26	27	28
29	30					

Today, we celebrate
Earth Day every year
in the month of April.

14

This holiday reminds
us to take good care
of our environment.

Like other holidays,
Earth Day can be a
time for celebrations.

Some towns have
festivals with music,
rides, and parades.

But the earth is still not
as clean as it could be.

The smog and garbage
have not gone away.

So on Earth Day, children
and adults around the
world do things to help
the environment.

20

Groups of people plant trees. Trees help keep the ground and the air healthy.

Some schoolchildren plant vegetable and flower gardens.

They help the gardens
grow with healthy plant
food. They do not use
chemicals (KEM-i-kuhls)
that can hurt the soil.

24

Many people start recycling (ree-SY-kling) programs to safely throw away plastic, paper, and glass.

These things do not go in the garbage.

Other people think of ways
to stop wasting water.

One way is to turn it off
while you brush your teeth.

Earth Day is not the only day when you can help make the environment clean and healthy.

You can do it every day of the year!

Words You Know

air

environment

smog

festival

30

garbage

garden

recycling

soil

water

31

Index

About the Author

David F. Marx is an author and editor of children's books.
He resides in the Chicago area.

Photo Credits

Photographs ©: AP/Wide World Photos: 13 (Steve Tomasko); Liaison Agency, Inc.: 4, 30 top right (Craig J. Brown), 5 (Alan Carey), 17, 30 bottom right (Porter Gifford), 3 (Lou Jr. Jacobs); Monkmeyer: 22, 31 top right (Dunn), 9 bottom, 30 bottom left (Sidney); PhotoEdit: 7 bottom (Cleo Photography), 23, 31 middle (Tony Freeman), 27 (Michael Newman), 20 (Elena Rooraid), cover, 7 top, 30 top left, (David Young-Wolfe); Stone: 6, 31 bottom right (Peter Cade), 10, 31 top left (Jay S. Simon); The Image Works: 23, 28, 31 bottom left (Bob Daemmrich), 15 (Syracuse Newspapers/David Lassman), 16 (F. Pedrick), 19 (Lisa Krantz), 9 top (Topham/UNEP).